Firing Cycle

Firing Cycle
50 Years of Clay at the Potters Guild

Firing Cycle
Copyright © 2000 by the Potters Guild, Ann Arbor
All rights reserved
Printed in the United States of America.
No part of this book may be used
or reproduced in any manner whatsoever
without written permission
except in the case of brief quotations
embodied in critical articles and reviews.
For information address
Historian, Potters Guild
201 Hill St.
Ann Arbor, Michigan 48104

First Edition

Catalog design by Adele Barres and Jeri Hollister
Potters Guild logo design by Maria Dickerman Carter

This book is printed on recycled paper

ISBN 0-9705553-0-X $12.00

Contents

What Is This Potters Guild?	2
Foreword	3
Acknowledgments	5
Who Were These Nine Founders of the Guild?	6
The Potters Guild- Memories Past and Present	9
The Golden Anniversary Show	28
Current Member's Work	29
Our Teacher's Work	43
Historical Work	53
The Plumer Collection	64
Fifty Years of the American Craft and the Potters Guild	67
Ode to the Guild	69
The Kilns	70
The Points System	73
Glaze Recipes from Our Teachers	78
Golden Anniversary Celebration	81
List of Members	82

WHAT IS THIS POTTERS GUILD?
By Sue Stoll (1978)

It is eighty
strong hands
and forty tired backs;

A shrine to clay,
beside the railroad track,
filled with potters' artifacts,
with a paid-off mortgage.

A mixed marriage of multi-talented
partners, welded for life by clay
and determination;

The senior citizen of local craft groups,
and prime mover in stimulating
awareness of pots 'n things.

ALL THAT AND MORE …

The Guild is a sort of democracy (with a bothersome
        set of rules to keep the democracy intact) –
and a kind of fraternity, whose headstrong personalities
        fight a little, talk clay a lot, eat, drink, and
        play together –
and a school to perpetuate the species –

and an idea exhange where fervor and passion
gently prod each potter to explore,
        expand,
              gamble,
                      refine,
                              and perfect –

BORN JUST A WORKSHOP, THE COMING OF AGE REVEALS –

An unshakable regard
for Guild before self –

A studio system so successful
it has been copied in distant places –

An idea that endured and surpassed
the wildest dreams of the nine founders
of an alley shop in 1949.

Foreword

by Jeri Hollister

This exhibition is the culmination of over a year of work on an idea that surviving and thriving for fifty years as a cooperative organization, is worth celebrating by telling others how it we did it. The exhibition is also a tribute to our founders and a gesture of gratitude for the inspiration and hard work of the members who built an organization that is alive and well a half-century after its conception.

Formed as a cooperative for ceramic artists in the summer of 1949, and legally incorporated in 1950, the Potters Guild in Ann Arbor, Michigan may be one of the oldest surviving cooperative workshops of its kind in the country. The studio serves over fifty members year round and up to 30 students every September through May. Ceramic classes are taught by members, local artists, and master of fine art students and graduates from the nearby university programs. Workshops are held approximately twice a year, bringing to the area accomplished artists who share their talents with the participants. The Potters Guild holds two exhibitions/sales per year on the premises, and has been involved in the Ann Arbor Street Art Fair since its inception 41 years ago.

We still have a founding member in the area, William Lewis, Professor Emeritus from the University of Michigan School of Art, and a small number of long time members who began to work at the Guild in its first decade. While we still have these valuable resources, we wanted to record some of the history of the Guild: how it was conceived, how it was organized, how it grew, and how it continues to function as a place where the craft is studied, taught and practiced. This catalog offers a compilation of thoughts and memories from present day Guild members. We are lucky to have members who began at the Guild in every decade since it was founded.

The exhibition itself consists of three parts. In the first section are **the works of the current members of the Potters Guild**. The work ranges from well designed hand made production pottery to sculptural works. The scale ranges from miniature pots less than one inch in diameter to multi-media pieces over six feet high.

The second section highlights **the current work of some of the Potters Guild's former teachers**. The Guild is fortunate to have had excellent artists teach its students. Those of you familiar with artists working in clay will recognize some names. This body of work exemplifies the range of ceramic art as well as other fine art being produced today.

In the third section are **works from the first twenty-five years at the Guild**. These works are by the founders of the Guild, artists working in clay who have taught a class or workshop at the Guild, and the work of members who were there between 1950 and 1975. In addition, we are showing a selection of pieces from the Plumer collection, a collection of Chinese and Korean pots and pot shards dating from the Han, Tang, Song and Ming dynasties (China) and Yi Dynasty (Korea) which were given to the Guild by James and Caroline Plumer.

Finally, we have included some information about the nuts and bolts of our cooperative. The Guild works for its members because every member works for the Guild, and the point system outlined in the first section of our catalog is at the core of how our cooperative functions. We present the system to you in its present incarnation. We have also included a section of favorite glaze formulas that were given to the Potters Guild by some of our teachers. The sharing of information is crucial to the spirit of cooperation.

We hope you enjoy the exhibition. The works on display illustrate the wealth of talent that has passed through the Potters Guild's studio, leaving a legacy that parallels the history of American ceramics in the second half of the twentieth century.

Acknowledgments

This catalog was made possible in part by a grant from
the Ventures Fund of the Minneapolis Foundation.

Additionally, the Potters Guild would like to acknowledge the generosity of those who helped fund the exhibition, this catalog, and other fiftieth anniversary events. They are listed in alphabetical order. There were a number of anonymous donations.

Private Donors:

Mr. and Mrs. Ted Bloodhart
Maria and Bill Carter
Sue and Richard Chase
Christine M. Comer
Gail and Jim Dapogny
Claudia and James Fairbanks
Ruth P. Freedman
Sally and Joel Goldberg
Dr. John and Suzan Hatch
Stephen T. Heald, D.D.S.
Jeri Hollister and Tom Bray
Gloria and Howard Lazar
Linda Lombardini
Jean Powell

Suzanne Powell, M.D.
P.J. Ryder and Donna Terek
Louis and Yvette Saravolatz
Milos and Anne Saravolatz
Lisa and Matthew Sevcik
Ellie and David Shappirio
Anna M. Smith
Jim Spevak
Steve Stefanac, D.D.S.
Marian (Terry) Titus
Stanley Watson and Huda Akil
Friedelle ad Jack Winans
Sue Woestehoff
Elaine Wolf
Charles Zill, D.D.S.

Corporate Donors:

CIGNA Foundation
Food Bytes, Tamara Castagna
The Home Depot, Ann Arbor
Merchant of Vino Marketplace
Minsky the Tailor
The Pizza House
Rovin Ceramics
Runyan Pottery Supply
Thomson-Shore, Inc.

Who Were These Nine Founders of the Guild? Impressions

By Ethel K. Potts

I called the Guild in 1950 to sign up for a sculpture class. They held a meeting, I was later told, to decide on whether or not to let the public into their classes, up to then held only for themselves.

Wilma Donahue

When I arrived at the Guild, only the founders were there. Dr. Wilma Donahue seemed to be the leader. As President she ensured decisions were made properly. mostly by consensus and that the group got along well together. A small woman with white hair twisted close to her head, she seemed very wise and professional. Bill Lewis thinks she had an interest in adult organizations – she was beginning her pioneering work in the new field of gerontology, and the Guild may have been an experiment for her. She must have done clay work at some early point, but I have no memory of seeing any pieces of clay on her hands. A busy person, we rarely saw her.

Harriet Waite

Harriet Waite was clearly the core person at the Guild, as Director. She was always there. She took care of the practical running of the place - supplies, utilities, rental matters, cleaning, equipment - everything, chores we have now split up among many members. On top of this she was the main fundraiser, with her many connections. She didn't stack or fire kilns, as I remember, but that was about all she didn't do. A small, sharp-minded woman with a long interest in art, she dressed with flair. I remember her purple velvet pants outfit, long before women wore pants regularly. Without Harriet, the Guild would have collapsed many times in the early years.

Ruth Lobdell

Ruth Lobdell had some U of M connection - a fraternity housemother? A faculty widow? I never knew. She and Harriet sometimes gossiped deliciously about University of Michigan people they both knew. (I'd stay quiet at my work so they'd forget I was there.) Ruth worked steadily at portrait busts or animal forms - sculpture only.

Eleanor LaPorte
Guilia Sunblad

Eleanor LaPorte and Guilia Sunblad were rarely at the Guild. I think the Guild was part of their general cultural interest more than a place to work. Eleanor and her husband had spent time in Japan, he as an advisor to Gen. McArthur. Both LaPortes became quite expert on Japanese art. Guilia did some sculpture, but I remember her mainly as a sophisticated presence, in her jodhpurs. (Jeans and pants were not available for women yet. Rather than wear farm overalls, I copied Guilia and wore riding jeans at the Guild.)

Harvey Littleton

By 1950, Harvey Littleton was no longer around the Guild as he was working full time at Cranbrook for an MFA. His contribution was earlier and major. With Bill Lewis he made our first wheels with stuff from Lansky's junk yard.

The two also used Ohio State University plans for a high fire globar electric kiln. Cone 9 and 10 oxidation firings were standard for us, with bisque and earthenware glazes fired together at cone 04. Those of the founders who threw learned early from Harvey. I watched him demonstrate only once but it was unforgettable - making large pots from small balls of clay. He threw thin and pulled all of the clay into the piece - little tooling was needed.

Bill Lewis

Bill Lewis was very much an early presence. For years Guild treasurer/secretary, his painting studio (and model train layout) were on the top floor of the building, and he walked through the Guild almost daily, stopping to talk, often about principles of design. The building would have been unaffordable without his sharing the rent. He also had the only phone in the building, which he shared. (The Guild still has his old phone number.) Bill's painting career was flourishing, so he no longer made many pots, though once a year he'd announce "It's time for my annual pot", and he'd throw a big punch bowl or jar. We all lent him glazes and fired the pot carefully, marveling at his continuing skill.

Hilda Burr
Carlos Palmer

All of the founders were unique characters, but the most unusual were Hilda Burr and Carlos Palmer. Hilda did scultpture, more memorable for the hours of work than for the results. She was an outspoken English woman, working at the University of Michigan in some field of psychology. She was undergoing analysis herself and she read Freudian significance into the forms we made. If we threw fat round forms or tall straight ones, she would look wise and say "Ahuummm". We became very self-conscious. Was there a shape she would not read as revealing? Square maybe? The tales she told were fun, and we missed her when she went back home. She felt disloyal not being in England while it was struggling after the war, though when she got there, she wrote: "life seems to consist of nothing but washing up".

Carlos spent a lot of time at the Guild, working on modern sculpture, carving geometric abstract forms. He also collected sculpture, as he could afford. (He gave U of M museum a good David Smith piece). Conversations were lively when he was present. He had wide interests, was an editor of the Middle English Dictionary, and both collected and wrote limericks, though he would not recite the most risqué ones when someone young, like me, was present. Too bad – they were hilarious.

The Potters Guild – Memories Past and Present

Compiled and Edited by Sally Goldberg

Today the Potters Guild studio bustles day and night with the activity of over fifty full and part-time potter-members, classes for thirty students, and a rigorous internship program. These pages tell the story of the Potters Guild's first fifty years in the voices of its members, past and present. Their collected memories resonate with pride of ownership, shared creativity, and feelings of joy at being part of both an artistically and financially successful cooperative studio, but also the vibrant community that is the Potters Guild.

The First Studio (1949 – 1963)

In late 1949, a group of nine Ann Arbor potters decided to rent a small studio in an alley off William and Maynard Streets, near the University of Michigan campus. The founders wanted the studio as both a workspace and learning space to which they could invite expert teachers to share their skills.

> *It's hard to believe the great teaching and the great pots that happened in the Guild's first primitive setting in the alley of William and Maynard streets. I think we relied on design knowledge and craft skills to make up for the inadequate facilities* **(Ethel (Eppie) K. Potts, the Guild's historian and its first student in 1950)**

Potters Guild, 1949-1963

How inadequate? Today's well-equipped Guild studio makes it difficult to recall the founders' shoestring budget, primitive conditions and scavenged equipment.

Bill Lewis, founding member

The equipment was produced at almost no cost... Out of a budget of $1200, only $500 of it went for equipment. That summer was spent cleaning out rubbish and restoring the old building. This involved installing a heating stove, a 220 voltage electric service, negotiating with the Carborundum Co. about special-order Globar kiln elements, building 3 momentum wheels from Lansky's junkyard stuff, and building the kiln from Ohio State plans. The skilled work was done by Bill Lewis and Harvey Littleton, who were inventing as they went along. Harriet Waite contributed the first $500, and the members paid dues of $100 a year. (**Bill Lewis, one of the nine founding members**)

By the fall of 1949 the Guild was ready for use. The workroom was smaller than our present wheel room, with our only sink, shelves and a toilet around the corner. A rickety low-ceilinged mezzanine was used for individual storage in orange crate shelves, and the basement for clay making and damp room. A wood stove for heat, no hot water, a simple spray booth. We made and stored our clay individually – sifting clay into water, then drying it in bats (**Eppie Potts**)

Guild Interior, 1949-1963

I remember mixing clay in the basement by hand, weighing glaze ingredients, washing my hands in cold water from the only tap, carrying my tools up to the mezzanine (It had a very shaky floor).

I felt relieved each time I returned safely to the main floor because we all expected the mezzanine to collapse at some time. The third floor was not especially useful because the stairway was so long and nothing above the first floor was heated. When several of us were invited to become members in about 1962 we had to climb all the way up there and sit around a table while we received our instructions.

Clay mixing, 1950s

Even the main floor was not very secure. The floor was quite bouncy and I caused one of the members to become angry when I slapped my clay on the wheel-head causing the floor to shake which caused the pot on the wheel next to mine to collapse. This was not unusual.

Then there was the toilet. It was at the bottom of the landing of the stairway. The concession to privacy was an extra door at the foot of the stairs that created a triangular enclosure. **(Ellie Shappirio)**

The toilet was in a problem location, at the bottom of the stairs going up. Two of the walls were doors - most people went in and pulled one door towards them, which left a gap. I remember, to be kind to newcomers, putting up signs saying "Hook A to A, and B to B, for privacy".

There were only three wheels, so sharing was necessary. They produced a soft clanking sound from the chains that controlled the sweep of the pedal. The kiln, housed in an attached garage, had a welded frame and door that took real strength to move. I did much of the stacking and firing, and had to push one foot against the nearby wall to get leverage to move it). **(Eppie Potts)**

But some things in Ann Arbor have changed little in fifty years…

Parking was difficult, making it hard to come to the Guild to work. We had no heat so kiln firing was very welcome in the winter. We had to keep our personal tools and things in a space in the loft, a dark and spooky place. **(Elaine Wolf)**

I remember JT Abernathy standing by our only sink, used for water supply and washing clay and glaze covered things. Knowing there was no clay trap and that we never needed to call a plumber, he scratched his head and said "you must have a straight pipe down to hell." **(Eppie Potts)**

Selling Pots – The First Sales and Art Fairs (1950s)

The Potters Guild's annual Spring and Christmas sales have been an Ann Arbor institution for decades. The Guild was one of the founders of the Ann Arbor Street Art Fair.

Ann Arbor Street Art Fair, 1960s

Though none of us were production potters, our pots were accumulating in our homes and sometime in the 1950s we thought we'd try holding a sale, using the alley in front of the Guild. We got permission from our landlady and alley owner, Mrs. Edith Nickels, whose backyard adjoined the alley. I remember her looking over her fence as the sale was underway and our bringing her a thank-you pot.

Guild alley sale, circa 1955

Inexperienced, we merely handed out a few flyers to friends and relatives, set up bricks with boards across, and made tasteful arrangements of some pots on the boards. We held half of the pots back in the Guild - if a pot sold, we would replace it with a suitable pot. That was the plan. Would anyone come? Would any pots sell? We peeked out the door and waited.

Within an hour, we had all the pots out –forget arrangements! Customers were looking for more. In a panic, as JT Abernathy remembers it, Bill Lewis or Charlie Meyers telephoned him and woke him up. "We're having a sale and need more pots."
(Eppie Potts)

Eager sales customers, circa 1970

In later years, with the sale an annual event, we decorated the alley with banners. We had learned that the public will buy our pots. Still later, we helped start the Street Art Fair on South University, with pots arranged along the curb and in front of stores. The rest is history, with the Guild's years of huge twice-annual sales, and the gigantic three street fairs dominating the city for four days in July every year. As one of the founding merchants said of the Street Fair, "This thing is snowballing into a mushroom". **(Eppie Potts)**

Potters Guild, circa 1963

A Building of Our Own (1963)

A decade passed, the Guild outgrew its cramped and primitive quarters and looked to purchase a building of its own. For a number of years, Guild members donated 50% of their sales to a building fund, and with some generous donations, raised the money to purchase the current studio. Installing the ceiling tiles in the new Guild seems to have been a memorable experience for all involved.

After much looking, we were fortunate to find 201 Hill which was Risdon Curry's nonferrous foundry. It had an industrial zoning, yet was near a residential neighborhood for safety, and in the middle of town for convenience. JT Abernathy remembers that the price was $16,500.

Buying the building, adding to it, and moving, were huge jobs... We completed major additions before we moved in - added the kiln room, bathroom, 2nd floor... I think the old Guild functioned somewhat until we moved, but after the move there was still a lot of work to do - painting, carpentry, assembling and installing shelving. Our contractor was persuaded to leave his scaffolding so we could install ceiling tile ourselves. I recall exhausting hours nailing over my head. **(Eppie Potts)**.

I also recall helping to nail the acoustical tiles to the ceiling before we moved in – definitely an unforgettable experience. **(Ellie Shappirio)**

I joined the Guild just a year or two before the big move to our own building. We all pitched in on the project – I nailed the ceiling tiles in place along with Marilyn Thayer and Larry McMahon. Many of us earned so many points that even the new facilities could never accommodate the resultant firings, so by mutual agreement we gave up the points. **(Maria Dickerman Carter)**

Sadly, there are no photos of the kiln being moved. Larry McMahon, in charge of the move, did not let us know when it would happen. It was by chance that I went to the Guild that morning just in time to see our kiln dangling high from a crane, moving very slowly down the State Street hill. What an archive or news photo it would have made! **(Eppie Potts)**

Potters Guild, 2000

I think I was president at the time and was in charge of settling in and starting up again. In l963, when we were ready, we held an Opening Ceremony, awarding "Hero of the Potters Guild" medals made by Bill Lewis, to those who had given hugely to the effort. As president, I ended the ceremony by throwing the first pot in the new Guild, signaling that it was permitted to work again. (**Eppie Potts**)

While I was Director we painted the entire building so the clay storage addition at the back looked like it belonged there. I remember Pauline Elliot holding the ladder while I painted at the very top of the building. None of us enjoyed heights…Later the Guild added on to the front of the building to accommodate more working space with supplemental funds from the Laura Vaughn memorial. Enlarging the studio opened more opportunity for students and members to attend workshops that were so vital in the growth of our Guild. (**Liz Davis**)

Laura Vaughn was a dear friend and a soul mate in art. She cared deeply for the Guild, and when she died, it was her wish that memorial funds go to the building of a new front for the Guild that would express the life of art and craft the building housed. I am proud that my husband, William T. Carter, as architect was able to help fulfill her wish. (**Maria Dickerman Carter**)

Making a Cooperative Work

Voicing principles of cooperation and non-discrimination, in 1950 the founders formally organized as The Potters Guild, a non-profit corporation. Most surprisingly, half a century later the Guild's original principles endure. These emphasize joint ownership, joint decision-making and the sharing of resources and knowledge, from taking turns on one-of-a-kind pieces of equipment to the sharing of clay techniques and glaze formulas.

Key to functioning in a cooperative is maintaining a balance on several levels, and ours is no different. The balance between individual focus and interacting is no small feat since we work in very close quarters, side by side, hour after hour. Long periods of solitary concentration bump up against conversations, laughter, radio, visitors, and phone calls… One common sight is members gathered around a piece by another member, discussing it. While routinely Guild members seek technical or aesthetic advice of others, unsolicited advice is also plentiful especially since a perplexed frown will almost always bring attention!

This is a byproduct of working in a cooperative, and ultimately, when one's skin becomes thick enough, it is recognized as a strong factor in one's artistic growth. I believe it works because underlying all communication is a mutual respect for one another. **(Gail Dapogny)**

But it wasn't always smooth sailing. After about ten years, the atmosphere of cooperation among the original members, often referred to as the "Guild Spirit", began to wane

Work for the benefit of the group - cleaning, stacking and firing kilns, bookkeeping, managing supplies, and so forth, was left to the few members who were conscientious about keeping the Guild going. They were assumed, hurtfully, to be potters with lesser talent. No wonder that major resentments and tensions built up. With some members never having time to make their own pots, we no longer liked or trusted each other. **(Eppie Potts)**

"There is a growing feeling that the Guild is a "service shop" where pots may be dropped off for firing and picked up later" **(Maxwell Reade's Director's Report, 1960)**

In the early 1960s, the membership charged a three-member committee of Jean Hazen, Janka McClatchey and Eppie Potts to find a way to rekindle the Guild Spirit. In a joint flash of inspiration, the committee pinpointed the key area of the potting process: every piece needed to be fired in the Guild's kilns. Based on this they invented the Points System, a way to enforce cooperation. **(Eppie Potts)**

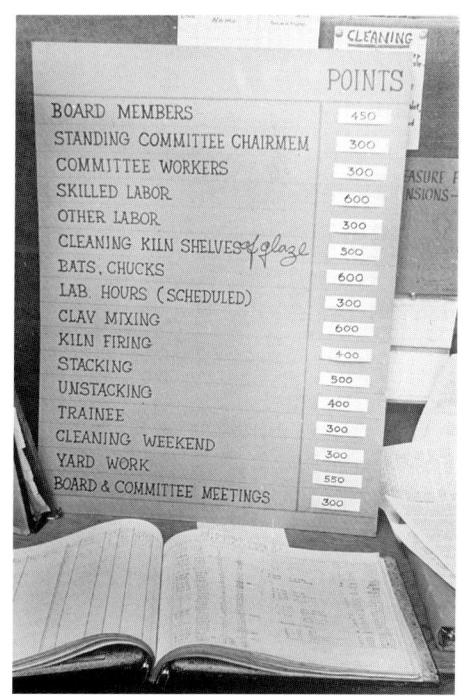

The Points System is simplicity itself. Members earn points by doing Guild work and trade in those points for space in the glaze kiln. One point of work earns 1 cubic inch of firing. Every task is rewarded with points, from serving as the Guild's elected President to keeping the floor free of clay dust. Members may not fire their pieces until they earn enough points **in advance** by working on behalf of the cooperative.

Points system

As I look back at my 49 years of membership in the Potters Guild I find I am proudest of my input to the Points System, as one of the three members of the committee that worked it out. Any other of my contributions pales beside that! (**Jean Hazen**)

The point system had been introduced by 1960, but some of the older members continued to do things as if it hadn't been. (**Ellie Shappirio**)

Another delicate balance point is between individual work and the ongoing needs of the physical Guild. Each member contributes to the labor and work that keep the Guild functioning such as making clay, loading and unloading kilns, firing, maintaining equipment, cleaning the guild, lugging heavy bags and materials. Everyone experiences times when Guild work seems to be an unwelcome intrusion, but generosity and discipline always prevail. Since members have keys, they can and do work at all hours — both Guild work and their personal work. It is common to see people working long into the night. If you're ever out for an early morning walk at 5 a.m. and peek into the Guild, you'll probably see Jeanette Powell conscientiously taking care of some task that needs attending. (**Gail Dapogny**)

Georgette Zirbes and class, 1970s

Teaching and Learning at the Guild

From its start in 1949, one of the Guild's major functions was to offer classes. A procession of illustrious potters taught Guild classes and workshops over the years, many just starting their careers as MFA graduates of the University of Michigan or Eastern Michigan University. Classes were opened to the public on a non-discriminatory first-come first-served basis, rotating students to serve as many people as possible. Most of today's Guild members started as students.

Its earliest three teachers were **Harvey Littleton** *and* **Mary (Kring) Risley** *(who both at the time were MFA students studying under Maija Grotell at Cranbrook), … and* **Ellen Colman-Bernkoff**, *an accomplished European-trained figurative sculptor. They shared everything they knew with founders/students and early classes…All of the early members took classes. That's why the Guild was created - for them to share teachers and studio.* **(Eppie Potts)**

In the winter of 1953 I visited the Guild out of curiosity and signed up for a course that would be 8 weeks long. **Rhoda (LeBlanc) Lopez** *was the teacher. We were required to master pinch-pot techniques for the first two weeks while I longed to try the potters wheels (We still have one of them – the one by the front window)… Rhoda was a stern teacher and I wasn't too impressed with her methods… We were told by Rhoda that she didn't want to see any brilliant blue pots after she introduced us to cobalt oxide. I still have mine.*
(Ellie Shappirio)

In l954 I got a chance to take a student course at the Guild with **J.T. Abernathy** *as instructor. This was wonderful although we hand-mixed our clay in basins in a cold basement. After forming our pots the effort proved worth it with the reward of seeing our pots in the final kiln!*
(Chuck Zill)

Rhoda Lopez, Charlene Fisher and JT Abernathy

Our teachers, Mary Kring and Rhoda LeBlanc Lopez encouraged us, after a year or so of classes, to send work to juried shows. The work of Guild members was accepted into the Syracuse Ceramic National, Michigan Artist-Craftsmen, Fiber-Clay- Metal, Designer-Craftsmen USA, as well as local juried shows and galleries. **(Eppie Potts)**

I began at the Guild as a student in the 1960s and one of my most memorable instructors was John Loree. He certainly taught me how to throw very thin pots ... to not waste energy centering clay that did not become an integral part of the piece. Tooling should only be the minimum. His use of rich surface decoration has had a strong influence on my work. (**Joan E. Otis**)

Shoji Hamada

Anna Smith *was my first teacher at the Guild. Her emphasis was creativity and her message was that there was more than one way to throw a pot. I was ready to be her student forever, however, she encouraged students to change teachers often so new ideas would be gathered. Later* **Wayne Higby** *and* **John Loree** *were good influences on my work. We had many memorable workshops especially when* (**Shoji**) **Hamada** *came to the Guild, I was reminded of an exciting class I took from Professor Plumer when a student at Michigan.* (**Liz Davis**)

About 1960 (after an absence from Ann Arbor) I decided to visit the Guild. I recall walking in and being greeted suspiciously by Isabella Liddell. After we established the fact that I had been a student years before, she allowed me to apply to take a course. My teachers were **Suzanne Stephenson, Nancy Plum, Gwaine Dart, Barbara Mansfield**, *and a man who was fired during our second class meeting by Louise (Piranian, Director) because he came in, went up to the third floor and stayed there during the whole class period. Some of my classmates were Sue Stoll, Harriet Larkin, Duncan McCarthy, Vee Ling Edwards, Bobbi Stevens, Larry McMahon and Heiju Oak.* (**Ellie Shappirio**)

I never forgot **Warren MacKenzie** *showing us how he moved a large pot from the wheel without distortion by placing a glossy paper on the top of his pot, capturing air inside and lifting it.* **Don Reitz** *said not to make a piece of junk permanent - refrain from firing it;* (**Liz Davis**)

Don Reitz

As an artist and art educator for 30 years, I appreciate having the Potters Guild as a resource for my own work and for clay students in Ann Arbor. It offers a community that provides camaraderie and support for claywork, a commitment to clay as a medium, and a high level of organization and thought towards making a collective clay studio work successfully. **(Debbie Thompson)**

After two semesters of ceramic classes I started working on my own at home. I tried for many years to make pots. Not until I took classes at the Guild did I find answers to my many questions. It has been the best experience I could ever hope for. My work has improved 100% since coming to the Guild. I love the feedback and get the opportunity to sell my work. Everyone is very friendly and supportive. I hope the Guild goes on forever. **(Joyce Friedrich)**

Becoming a Guild Member

In the early years, new and potential potters were eagerly welcomed as Guild members, with the membership process being – to say the least — easy and informal.

The Guild needed to grow in working hands and funds. Early new people were invited to membership almost as soon as they signed up for classes. Jean Hazen remembers that Carrie Taylor and Winnie Arnold (Ramfjord) were already members when she arrived. Soon after, I remember Dorothy Cahill and Louise Weatherford as members. All of the early members took classes, wheel taught by Mary Kring (Risley) and sculpture taught by Ellen Colmar Bernkoff. That's why the Guild was created - for them to share teachers and studio.
(Eppie Potts)

My first introduction to the Guild was through Janka McClatchey, who was a Potters Guild member. At that time there was no way to officially apply as a permanent member. You just hoped that some member would bring your name up at a meeting. If you were voted in, that was it. **(Shirley Knudsvig)**

Guild interior, 1960s

Today, a membership application does not automatically lead to acceptance. Limited space on the personal storage shelves restricts the number of new members the Guild can accommodate. Prospective members most commonly have been students and then run the gauntlet through a two-year internship before becoming eligible for election to permanent Guild membership. The thrill of finally being accepted into this artistic community often evokes strong emotions of jubilation. For many members, it signifies a pivotal point in their lives.

> *I remember that all-important phone call late in the evening of June 10, 1973. It was the Potters Guild's spring meeting, and membership was on the agenda. I was a fourth term student in the Guild, and longed to become a member. For hours, I busied myself around the house with inane tasks until finally, giving up all pretense of cool indifference, I sat and stared fixedly at the phone, alternating between hope and despair, willing it to ring. And it happened! My friend, the Guild's membership chairman, Shirley White-Black, called with the news and sounded genuinely touched by my excitement. I laughed, and babbled, and hugged Jim, and hugged our dog, and even shed some tears, until I finally had to hop in the car and drive by the Guild, just to give it all reality.* **(Gail Dapogny)**

> *Initially classes were organized for members. It was much later, with public demand for classes, that members were invited only if they could work independently, not take up class space. That is when workshops started to keep members stimulated, because unlike the early days, we no longer had the inspiration of watching our teachers do their own work at the Guild.* **(Eppie Potts)**

Guild interior, 2000

I was thrilled when I was voted into membership. However, after being in charge of purchasing with Gerry Grygotis for a couple of years and then serving as Director, and later as President of the Guild, I realized the advantages of being a student. (**Liz Davis**)

I started at the Guild as a student about ten years ago and recently was accepted as a full member. I was thrilled when I got the news that I had been voted in – I had been yearning for this moment for years. That night, my husband and I had a special celebratory dinner with champagne! I had to call and tell everyone the good news. No longer a student, as a member, I feel I still have access to the finest teachers, mentors, and friends. (**Sally Goldberg**)

The Guild as a Community

The Guild is much more than a cooperative pottery studio. In addition to being a place where ideas and techniques are shared, it is a nurturing community of fellow artists and good friends.

The Guild is a well-equipped studio, which promotes diversity in ceramic creation and community among its members. Its educational component promotes the diversity and tests the values, techniques and aesthetics of everyone. (**Jeanette Powell**)

Certainly the "Glaze Box" full of members' glaze recipes to share was a very important help for new students and Guild members alike. So many times when I was a new student, a member would offer help and advise as we were sitting at our wheels throwing pots. The enthusiasm, encouragement and friendliness I encountered at the Guild are among my fondest memories. **(Madelaine Gault Conboy)**

It is difficult to summarize all that the Guild has meant to me but three things certainly stand out: professional growth, friendship and community. **(Shirley Knudsvig)**

Occasionally personalities clashed (are you surprised?) and some people preferred not to work when certain others were there. Somehow, I haven't been conscious of that sort of thing since we moved. Maybe because all of us are more professional and adult! As for what the Guild has given me during these years ... many friends, many moments of support, challenges, opportunities, inspiration - and especially the chance to put my hands in clay. There has been no other organization in my life equal to the Guild. **(Jean Hazen)**

In celebrating its 50th Year, the Guild can take credit for having given an opportunity to so many who might never have found their uniqueness and pleasure working in the medium of clay. Clearly, 50 years is unquestionable evidence of this successful cooperative organization. **(Liz Davis)**

I feel truly privileged to be a part of this dynamic ceramics community. Knowledgeable colleagues are always willing to share their expertise. **(Sally Goldberg)**

Clay mixing, 2000

My exposure to the Guild was first as a teacher, then as a resident potter, a workshop presenter, and finally a member so I've seen it from several perspectives Each type of contact has reinforced my impression of an organization with plenty of rules to follow but also full of people willing to have their eyes opened to different points of view. For example, after being a member for a while, I had a pet snake (George) who died and so I cast him into a piece and didn't think to tell anyone about it. When the piece came out of the bisque I was commenting about glazing George and there was a silence for a minute or two while everyone around me took this in. Bobbi Stevens then told me that I should have warned the kiln firers that there was organic matter in the bisque so they would know where the strange smell was coming from during the firing. It was a good joke at the Guild for a while. **(Adele M. Barres)**

When I was asked to join the Guild in February of 2000 as an adjunct member, my heart exploded with joy. I felt so honored to be part of a group that I had admired for so long. I expected to be working alongside potters with vast experience in throwing, hand building, glazing, and all aspects of the craft. What I didn't expect was to be treated so warmly by kind, sensitive, humorous, well educated, well traveled, and a generally good group of folks that will be friends for life. From the moment I set foot in the Guild, I have felt accepted and nourished. Knowing how to make a stranger feel welcomed and part of a family is a portion of what these special people have learned through their 50 years as The Potters Guild. **(Susan Salmeron)**

Glaze area, 2000

Potters Guild members, 2000

Perhaps Gail Dapogny best describes the Guild community:

> It's almost as though the Guild has special radar when it comes to selecting prospective members who will merge comfortably and productively within its organization. The talent is abundant, the diversity impressive, the energy high. Yet, with all the energy driving this group of strong personalities, the compatibility and mutual acceptance is remarkable. We share the peculiarly intimate friendship of people used to working together over years. Eventually we come to know and accept each other's habits, foibles, strengths and weaknesses, as well as spouses, kids, grandkids, parents, dogs and cats. We gain members, and sadly, we lose members, but somehow the Guild maintains its special character.
>
> Very much a part of the Guild is a compassion and sensitivity extraordinary in such a large group. Once, long ago, when I was feeling upset over some small issue, my friend Ellie Shappirio, observing this, came over and hugged me. She said to me, quite simply, "You'll never come closer than you do here to having a big group of sisters and brothers who sometimes quarrel but always, always care about each other. Don't forget that." And I didn't.

Another example for me of the Guild's strong support base includes a period of years when I ran into health difficulties, resulting in a number of lengthy hospital stays and surgeries. The Guild kept me plied with continual, reassuring phone calls, notes, and at least one visit each day from various members. It was enormously touching, and I realized how very much indeed this was my "other" family. Others in the Guild who suffer losses or trauma also discover the strong support of this group of friends.

Another point of balance at which we excel: combining work and play! When 4 p.m. rolls around, stomachs begin to growl and the subject turns to food and dinner. Occasionally a bottle of wine materializes, and we have an instant, spontaneous party.

There is ample justification for the notion that the Guild can solve all problems. We are a human database of information and experience, and collectively, we are anything but shy about tapping into it. We take on all issues: child-rearing, house repair, music, landscaping, dog training, golf, science—all fields; we tackle travel plans, orchid-raising, how to handle city council, what to cook for an upcoming dinner party. (What we can't answer, we take home to our spouses.) What a rich and interesting background lurks behind all those splendid pots!

So, with all this diversity, what brings us together? Well, of course, it is our love of clay, our fiercely serious commitment to making works of clay. We are mutually yet individually consumed by questions of form, design, clay consistency, glaze results, firing effects. Clay is our common denominator, our language.

What you see in this (Slusser Gallery) show is the amazing variety, the solid craftsmanship, and the wonderful creativity of a very special group of friends, past and present, who have figured out how to work together, how to keep growing individually, and how to combine strong successful traditions, honed over fifty years, with fresh ideas. To put it more simply, the Potters Guild works. **(Gail Dapogny)**

The Golden Anniversary Show
Photographs by Jeri Hollister
(unless otherwise noted)

	pages
Current Members' Work	29 - 42
Our Teachers' Work	43 - 52
Historical Work	53 - 63
The Plumer Collection	64 - 66

Current Members' Work

JT Abernathy
Sea Anemone, 1999, Stoneware
h 23.25" dia 17"

Beverly Allport
Tall Jar, 1999, Raku
h 16" dia 6"

Penelope Barlow
Keramos, 2000, White Stoneware
h 15" w 24" d 3.5"

Adele Barres
Untitled, 2000, White Stoneware
h 17" w 13" d 15"

Mary Blanton
Large Bowl, 1996, Porcelain
h 5.5" dia 11.5"

Cindy Wolf Campbell
Shino Teapot, 2000, Stoneware
h 6" w 9.25" d 7.5"

Maria Dickerman Carter
Shibui II, 1999, White Stoneware
h 17" w 14.5" d 4.5"

Sue Chase
Variations on a Theme from Senegal, 2000,
White Stoneware
average h 4.5", base w 10.5" d 5.25"

Jim Clark
Miniature Jar, 1987, Porcelain
h 0.625" dia 0.625

Jane Connin
Boxes Born of Fire and Ash, 2000, Porcelain
left to right: (1)h 5" w 4" d 4"
(2)h 4" w 4" d 3.5"
(3)h 4.5" w 3.5" d 3.75"

Debby Cocoros
Indian Woman, 2000
Raku, Casino Chips
and Wood
h 82" w 14.75" d 6.5"

Gail Dapogny
Black Box II, 2000
Porcelain and Wood
h 29.5" w 8.5" d 4.75"

Liz Davis
Plate with hole, no date, Porcelain
h 1.25" dia. 7.5"

Royce Disbrow
Untitled, 1999, Clay Print
h 13" w 19"

Ryan Forey
Vessel, 1999, Stoneware
h 9.75" w 5.5" d 5.5"

Joyce Friedrich
Covered Jar, 2000, White Stoneware
h 7.75" dia 8.5"

Sally Goldberg
African Influenced Mask, 2000, Raku
h 22.5" w 10.5" d 2"

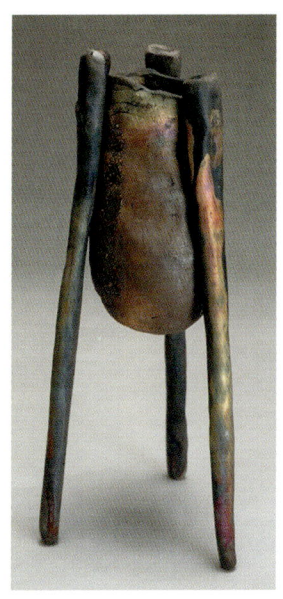

Nancy Grob
Tripod, 2000, Raku
h 11.75" w 5.25" d 5"

Jean Hazen
Carved Bowl, 1985, Stoneware
h 9.5" dia 11.25"

Jeri Hollister
Large Iron Tribute, 98-26, 1998
Earthenware, h 46" w 34" d 11"

Loretta Jenkins
Jar, 1955, Stoneware
h 6.25" dia 4.75"

Shirley Knudsvig
Pair of Dancers, 2000, Raku
left: h 15.75" w 14" d 5.5"
right: h 15.5" w 10.75" d 5.5"

Will Laycock
Adam and Eve Series, 2000, White Stoneware
left to right: (1)h 12.5" w 3" d 2"
(2)h 10.5" w 2" d 2"
(3)h 12" w 3.25" d 2.5"
(4)h 9" w 3.5" d 4.25"

Gloria Lazar
Untitled, 2000, White Stoneware
h 13.5" w 14.5" d 13.5"

Dorothy Levin
Round Platter, 2000, Stoneware
h 3.5" dia. 18"

Ed Lindberg
Bowl, 1990, Stoneware
h 3" dia 9"

Rebecca Liu
Copper Red Plate, 1999, White Stoneware
h 2" w 12" d 12"

Susan McKinney
Bowl, 2000, Stoneware
h 4" dia 16"

Inge Merlin
Plate, 1999, White Stoneware
h 2" dia 12.75"

Roann Ogawa
Platter, 2000, White Stoneware
h 3" w 13" d 14"

Joan E. Otis
The Water Hole, 2000, White Stoneware
h 13.75" w 14" d 8.5"

Louise Piranian
Three Bowls, 2000, Porcelain
h 3.75" dia 5" each

Ethel K. Potts
Memorial Stone, 1999, Stoneware
h 14" w 12" d 2"

Jeanette Powell
Bird Bath, 2000, White Stoneware
h 32.5" dia 22"

Jan Powers
Table with Vase, 1992,
Earthenware
h 37.5" w 21" d 22.25"

Donna Rea
Plate, 1985, Porcelain
h 3.25" dia 14"

I.B. Remsen
Vessel with Tall Handle, no date
White Stoneware and Wood
h 24" w 9.5" d 9.5"

Cher Rusling
Flying Pot, 1999, Stoneware
h 10.75 w 11 d 7

Susan Salmeron
Lidded Vessel, 2000, Earthenware and Petrified Wood
h 7" w 11" d 11"

Deb Saravolatz
Drum, 2000, Porcelain
h 13.75" w 8.25" d 7.75"

Ena Schlorff
Faceted Teapot, 1999, Porcelain
h 6" w 8" d 6"

Jim Schulz
Light, 1999, Stoneware
h 30" dia 9"

Ellie Shappirio
Two Plates with Inlaid Glaze, 1999, Porcelain
h 2" dia 10"

Brian Smith
Platter, 1999, Stoneware
h 7" dia 21"

Denise Smith
Square Vessel, 1996, Stoneware
h 5.5" w 10" d 10"

Jim Spevak
Untitled, 1999, White Stoneware
h 1.5" dia 12"

Steve Stefanac
Saggar-Fired Jar, 1997, Porcelain
h 6.25" w 5.5" d 4.5"

Bobbi Stevens
Urban Nightfall, 2000, Raku
h 46" w 17.5" d 3"

Sue Stoll
Platter, 2000, Porcelain
h h 1.75" dia 19"

Sarah Taggart
Figure, no date, low fire clay
h 16.5" w 6" d 9.5"

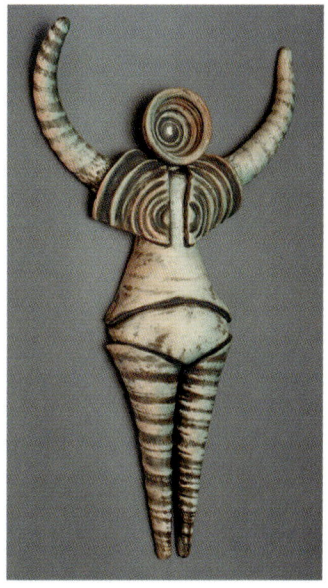

Debbie Thompson
Female Figure, 1999,
Porcelain
H 14" w 8.5" d 2"

Terry Titus
Fallen Warrior, 1990, Terra Cotta
h 7" w 25" d 8"

Shirley White-Black
Untitled, 1999, White Stoneware
h 21.5" w 14.75" d 7.25"

Friedelle Winans
Bowl, 2000, White Stoneware
h 6" w 6" d 4.5"

Elaine Wolf
Cups, 2000, Porcelain
left to right: (1)h 6" dia 3.25", (2)h 4.25" dia 3.5"
(3)h 5" dia 3.25". (4)h 4.25" dia 3.5"

Jin Young Yeum
Jar, 1999, Raku
h 12" dia 5"

Chuck Zill
Slip Decorated Plate, 1990, Stoneware
h 2.5" dia 11"

Our Teachers' Work

Pi Benio
Haystack Trilogy, 2000, Pit Fired White Stoneware
each piece: h 10" x w 3" x d 2.5"
Photograph by Brain Steele

J. Robert Black, Jr.
Vessel, 1993, Raku
h 10" dia 12"
Photograph by J. Robert Black, Jr.

Ed Brownlee
Untitled, 2000, Stoneware, h 9" w 6" d 6"
Photograph by Ed Brownlee

Susan Crowell
Lust and Gluttony from Seven Deadly Sins series,
1999, Salt-fired Porcelain
h 4.5" dia 2.75"

Gawaine Dart
Solstice Jar, 1987, Stoneware
h 24" dia (excluding handles) 7.5"

Maxwell Davis
Lunar Table, 2000, Hot and Cold Glass
h 21.5" dia 16.25"

Rafael Duran
la pesadilla de un alfarero, 1993-2000
Clay and Wood, h 24" w 15" d 6"

Diane Erickson
Translucent Alignment, 2000,
Stoneware, Wood, Glass, Feathers,
Rocks, Wicker, Silk Plant
h 31" w 20" d 18"

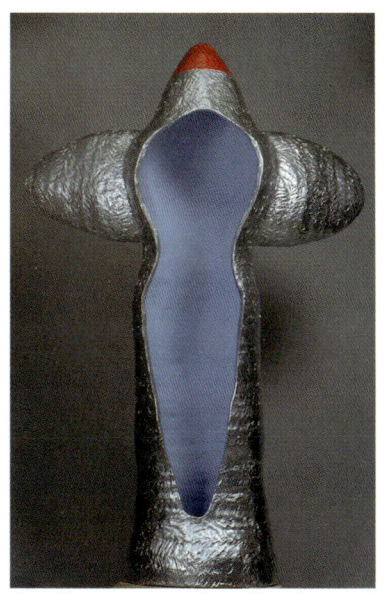

Sandra Ginter
Suit Al., 2000, Ceramic
h 6'8" w 4'3" d 2'
Photograph by Sandra Ginter

Emmerson Greenman
Vessel, 1987, Porcelain
h 3.75" dia 4"

Karen Gunderman
Spare Parts #4 Gametes, 1999, Castable
Refractory, Porcelain and Wood
h 30" w 24" d 5"
Photograph by Chris Davis-Benavides

Wayne Higby
Corridor Gap, 1999, Raku-fired Earthenware
h 8" w 8.5" d 4"
Photograph by Brian Oglesbee

Skip (Fred) Hunter
Remembering Peep, 1999
Pewter, Copper, Wood and Silk
h 7" w 5.75" d 5.75
Photograph by Skip Hunter

Gail Kendall
Tureen, 2000, Terra Cotta
h 14" dia 14"
Photograph by Roger Bruhn

Ned Krouse
Wall Bowl, 1998, Raku, h 3.5" dia 18"
Photograph by Ned Krouse

Deb LeAir
Untitled, 1999, Earthenware, h 13" dia 6"
Photograph by Larry Sanders

Yiu-Keung Lee
memoir, chapter 1, 2000, Salt-fired stoneware
each unit: h 12" w 9" d 1.5"
Photograph by Yiu-Keung Lee

Tom McClure
Figure in Harem, 1986, Oil on Canvas
h 30" w 40"

David Mac Donald
Middle Passage #1, 1996,
Earthenware, h 24" w 14" d 8"
Photograph by Brantley Carroll

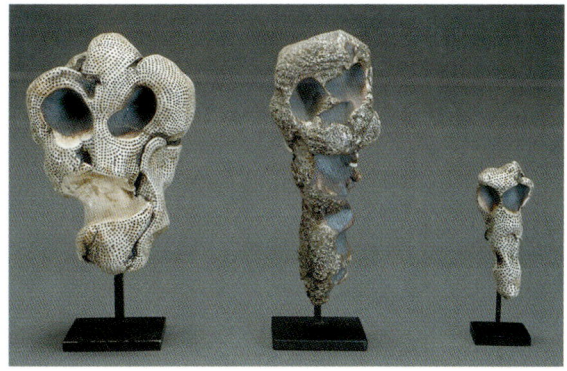

Michele Oka Doner
3 Sperm Skulls, 1990's, Porcelain
L to R: (1) h 7.75" l 4.25" d 3.5",
(2) h 8" l 2.75" d 2.25", (3) h 4.75" l 1.5" d 1"

Michael Padgett
Spill Vase Figure, 1999
Ceramic
h 18" w 7" d 6"
Photograph by
Michael Padgett

David Parsons
Speak No Envy, 1990's, Earthenware
h 20" w 19" d 16"

Tom Phardel
Vessel, 1999, Salt-fired Stoneware
h 9" w 21" d 11"

Nancy Manes Plum
Covered Jar, 2000, Ceramic, h 9" dia 7"
Photograph by Jens Plum

Robert Piepenburg
Vase, 1999, Raku
h 10.5" dia 7"
Photograph by Robert Piepenburg

Rick Pruckler
Reclining Figure, 2000, Ceramic and Steel
Length 14"
Photograph by Rick Pruckler

Jackie Rice
Teapot, no date, Porcelain
h 9.75" w 7.5" d 6"

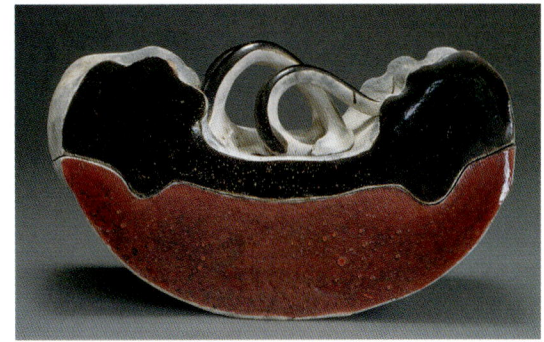

Helga Schmerl Haller
Baroque Box, 1970, Raku
h 10.75" w 19" d 7"

Daniela Richter
Untitled, c. 1990, Stoneware
h 49.5" w 10" d 11"

Sandra Dalton Shaughnessy
Platter, 2000, Cone 10 Soda Fired
h 2" w 13.5" d 7.5"

Annette Siffin
Pitcher, 2000, Stoneware
h 10.5" w 9" d 6.75"

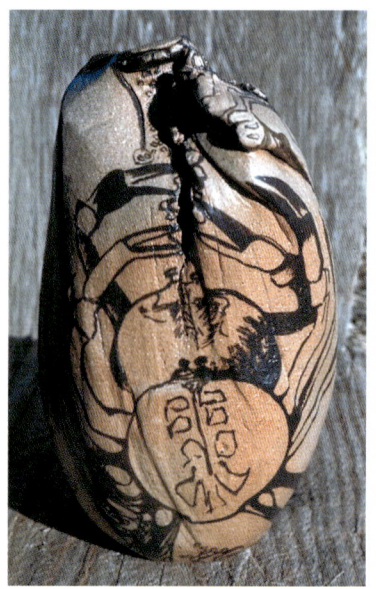

Anna Smith
Purse Crabs, c.1985, Stoneware
h 9" w 5" d 3.5"
Photograph by Anna Smith

John Stephenson
Zone Three, 1999, Terra cotta
h 21.75" w 27.25" d 3.25"
Photograph by John Stephenson

Susanne Stephenson
Gorge Rush II, 1999, Terra cotta
h 30" w 23" d 7"
Photograph by John Stephenson

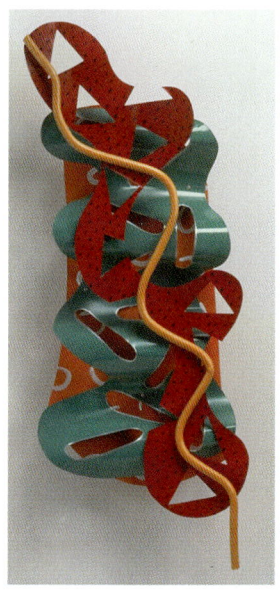

Andreé Valley
Vertical Wave II, 1998, Painted
Aluminum, h 42" w 16" d 8"
Photograph by Bill Fritsch

Tom Venner
Graft 2, 2000, Clay and Wood, h 20"
Photograph by Tom Venner

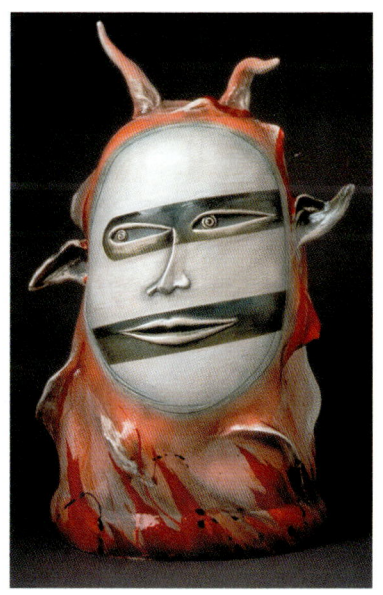

Pat Warashina
Hot Head, 1993, Ceramic
h 25.5" w 16" d 14"
Photograph by Roger Schreiber

Sandra Westley
W. 21 Road, 1999/2000, Low-fire Nebraska Clay
and Adobe Bricks, h 7" w 69" d 69"
Photograph by Sandra Westley

Jane White
Reclamation Series, 1999, Fired Clay and Glaze
Materials Mounted on Metal Plates
Each Unit: h 14" w 9.25" avg. d 4"

Suzanne Wolfe
Speciman/Sentinel, 1997,
Ceramic and Bronze, h 9.5"
Photograph by Brad Goda

Marie Woo
Untitled, 1999, Ceramic, 18" dia
Photograph by Marie Woo

Georgette Zirbes
Krumlov Conversations #9, 1999, Ceramic
h 18" w 18" d 5.5", Photograph by G. Zirbes

Historic Work

Jeri Hollister

The work you see in the *Historic Work* section of our exhibition comes from the Potters Guild's first 25 years. These works are by the founders of the Guild, artists working in clay that taught a class or workshop at the Guild, and the work of members working between 1950 and 1975. You will see names that have become part of the canon of artists working in clay in the twentieth century. Among them are the works of **Wayne Higby**, **Bernard Leach**, **Warren MacKenzie, Michele Oka-Doner, John Stephenson,** and **Pat Warashina**. One founder whose clay work is shown here, **Harvey Littleton** has often been called the father of American glass. The bronze works of two early teachers, European artist **Ellen Colmar/Bernkoff** and **Tom McClure**, Professor Emeritus from the University of Michigan School of Art, illustrate that the founders and early members were interested in sculpture as well as the more traditional ceramic arts.

We decided to show a selection of work from the early years of the Guild to pay a tribute to the members whose vision and hard work laid the foundation on which today's Guild was built. The high aesthetic quality of the work puts into context the place the Potters Guild holds in the development of craft in the United States during the second half of the twentieth century.

J.T. Abernathy
Bottle, no date, Stoneware
h 8.25" dia 4.5"

Fred Bauer and Pat Warashina
Casserole, late 1960s
Stoneware
h 5" dia 11"

J. Robert Black
Slab Vase, 1960s, Stoneware
h 8" w 6" d 2.5"

Jo Carter
Jar, c. 1965, Stoneware
h 7.5" dia 9"

Maria Dickerman Carter
Vase, c. 1975, Raku
h 13.5" w 14" d 4"

Mary Chuang
2 Part Vessel, c. 1975, Stoneware
h 12.25" w 11" d 7.25"

Ellen Colmar/Bernkoff
Figure, early 1950s, Bronze
h 4.5" w 5" d 7"

Larry Cronk
Small Faceted Jar, c. 1965, Stoneware
h 4.5" dia 3.5"

Vee Ling Edwards
Teapot, no date, Stoneware
h 5" w 6.25" d 5.25"

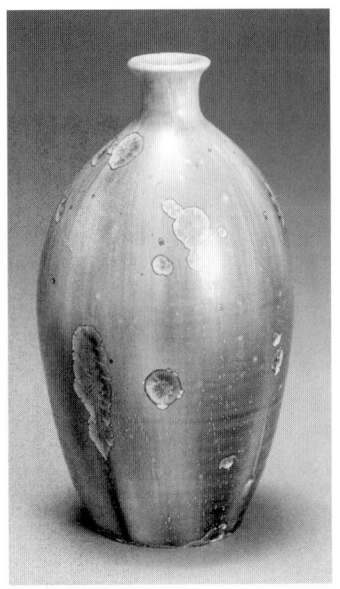

Pauline Elliot
Bottle with Crystaline Glaze,
1970s, Porcelain
h 7" dia 3.5"

Charlene Fisher
Untitled, 1960s, Stoneware
h 13" w11.75" d 5.5"

Jean Hazen
Bottle with dripping Glaze, 1955, Stoneware
h 9" dia 10"

Jim Heinonen
Cat Lantern,
1970-75, Stoneware
h 10.5" dia 7"

Wayne Higby
Plate, 1960s, Raku
h 2.25" dia 10"

Bernard Leach
Vessel, 1950s, Stoneware
h 5.75" dia. 6"

William Lewis
Bowl, 1955, Stoneware
h 5" dia. 11.25"

Harvey Littleton
Bowl, 1950s, Stoneware
h 3.25" dia 10.75"

Richard Lincoln
Round Bottle, 1956, Stoneware
h 10" dia. 9.5"

Ruth Lobdell
Baboon, no date, Stoneware
h 9.5" w 4.5" d 8.25"

Rhoda and Carlos Lopez
Plate w/Three-Headed Bird, 1950s, Stoneware
h 2" dia 15.75"

John Loree
Goblet, 1960s, Stoneware
h 9.75" dia 4"

Tom McClure
Ecliptic, 1963, Bronze
h 30" w 22" d 9"

Warren and Alix MacKenzie
Bottle, 1960s, Stoneware
h 3.75" dia 3.5"

Charles Meyers
Lidded Jar, 1950s, Stoneware
h 6.5" dia 5"

Bill Morgan
Plate, 1950, Stoneware
h 1" dia 8.75"

Alice Mulchahey
Tiny Bowl, early 1970s, Stoneware
h 1"

Michele Oka Doner
Untitled, 1960s, Porcelain
h 5.5" w 10" d 8"

Nancy Manes Plum
Lidded Jar, 1950s, Stoneware
h 8.25" dia 8"

Ethel K. Potts
Untitled, 1954, Stoneware
h 6" w 13.5" d 10.5"

Margaret Runkel
Bowl with Turquoise Interior, 1950-55, Stoneware
h 3.25" dia 9"

Nick Prokos
Vessel, c. 1960, Stoneware
h 8.75" w 8.75" d 4.25"

Maxwell Reade
Bottle, 1960, Stoneware
h 7.5" dia 4"

Mary Kring Risley
Bottle with Scorpions, 1952,
Stoneware, h 11.75" dia 7"

Kurt Schneider
Bottle with Applied Decoration,
c. 1960, Stoneware
h 7.75" dia 6.5"

John Stephenson
Tall Bottle, 1950s, Stoneware
h 19.25" w 10.5" d 10"

Terry Titus
Bottle, 1957, Stoneware
h 14" w 12" d 10.75"

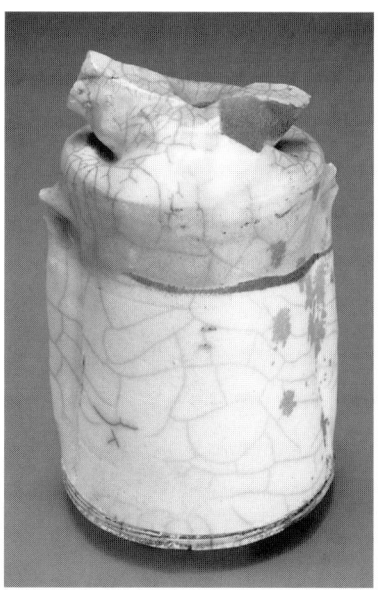

Laura Vaughn
Bottle, 1960s, Raku
h 10" dia 6.5"

Harriet Waite
Vessel with Cat decoration, c. 1950,
Stoneware
h 4.75" dia 3.5"

Pat Warashina
Lidded Ball, 1960s, Stoneware
h 12" dia 10"

Elaine Wolf
Water and Earth, 1960s, Stoneware
h 3.75" dia 18"

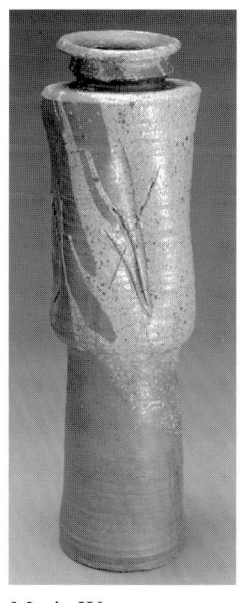

Marie Woo
Tall Vase, 1950s, Stoneware
h 19" dia 6.25"

Donna Zajonc
Two Cups, 1975, Porcelain
left h 3" w 4" d 3", right h 2.5" w 4.5" d 3.75"

The Plumer Collection

Ethel K. Potts and Jeri Hollister

These ceramic works have been selected from a body of work given to the Guild by James and Caroline Plumer. James Plumer was Professor of History of Art at the University of Michigan. He and his wife Caroline were friends of the Guild. From his work in China and Korea he brought back an extensive collection of art objects and artifacts. Many of the museum quality pieces are housed in the University of Michigan Museum of Art. To the Guild he and his wife gave those pieces that only potters would understand and value; beautiful shards, kiln accidents, fused stack of bowls, and stuck "buttons".

There are artifacts from China that date from the seventh to the seventeenth centuries, and a group from Korea dating from the eighteenth century. Housed in the Guild's permanent collection, these wonderful treasures are available for members and students to hold and examine thereby gaining a deeper knowledge and appreciation for the craft.

Temmoku group, bowls and saggar
1200-1299 (Southern Song Dynasty, 1127-1279, to Yuan Dynasty, 1280-1368)
saggar h 5.75", bowls dia. 5"

Qing Hui ware
960-1279 (Song Dynasty)
dia. 6.75"

Yue ware (proto-celadon), fragments and oil jar
618-907, Tang Dynasty
largest dimension 5.5"

Celedon fragments
1368-1644 (Ming Dynasty)
largest dimension 10.75"

Round fragment and pitcher
10th century (Late Tang/early Song Dynasties)
fragment dia. 3.25", pitcher h 8"

Small bowls
no date
dia. 3.25" each

Yue sagger
6th-7th century (Late Han Dynasty)
largest dimension 8.5"

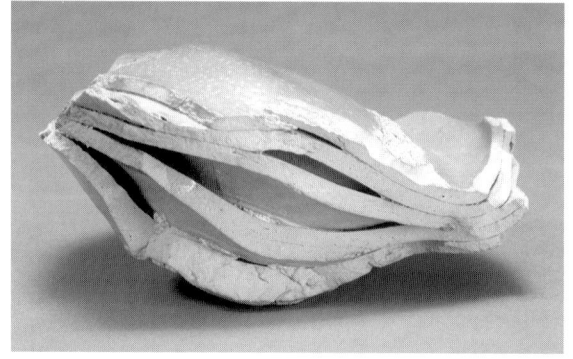

Yue ware, collapsed bowls
6th-7th century (Late Han Dynasty)
largest dimension 6"

Korean pot shards
18th century, Yi Dynasty (1392-1910)
largest dimension 8"

Fifty years of the American Craft World and the Potters Guild

By Ethel K. Potts

In our 50 years we at the Guild have had a chance to observe and to be part of the development of the American clay art world. Fifty years ago we were aware that there were major clay programs at some universities and schools such as Ohio State, Cranbrook, and Claremont College. "A Potters Book" by Bernard Leach was relatively new and was having a strong influence on clay firing, decoration, and especially on glazes. Our first stoneware glazes were largely Temmoku, Kaki, and basic ash glazes, and our first decorations were brush strokes and layering of glazes, both from Leach.

While we admired the relaxed warmth of the oriental forms shown by Leach, we were being taught, as were most Americans, from the European and Scandinavian tradition – controlled, rigid, with no signs of human hands. Our earliest teachers were trained in Europe or under Maija Grotell at Cranbrook. These teachers were either established in or moving into the gallery/juried show world: **Ellen Colmar Bernkoff** with sculpture, and **Rhoda (LeBlanc) Lopez** with large commission pieces. **Mary (Kring) Risley**, herself a graduate student at Cranbrook along with **JT Abernathy** and **Harvey Littleton**, was testing her own work in juried shows. As Kring's student, I remember her vigorous teaching, driving us, as she drove herself, to high design and clay skills. After two or three Guild semesters, she helped us select and send works to shows, as part of our learning experience.

Slowly in the 1950s, juried art shows were beginning to include crafts: the Ann Arbor Art Association's Members Annual, the Detroit Institute of Arts Michigan Artists' Craftsman Annual, shows in Kalamazoo, Bay City, and Midland. Most exciting were the national shows devoted to crafts. In 1951, Kring encouraged a number of us to send pieces to the Syracuse Ceramic National and five of us had works accepted. Excited, we filled a car and drove to the opening, and were kindly given a preview. Some Guild potters continued sending to shows for years, sometimes being awarded various prizes, including purchases by museums.

A few Guild members continued to be part of the growing display of crafts in national and invitational shows, including such shows as American Crafts Council's Young America, in New York, Midwest Designer-Craftsmen, Fiber-Clay-Metal, Designer Craftsmen USA, and Michigan Ceramics. Those of us who showed became expert at packing and shipping.

Clay art and other crafts have risen to a major place in the art world with such huge shows as SOFA (Sculpture, Objects and Functional Art), ACC (American Craft Council), filled with craftsmen represented by major galleries. Crafts now can be large, serious, and expressive as only painting and sculpture used to be.

The market for selling crafts did not develop until the 1960s. Previously some Guild members could sell a few pieces through the Forsythe Gallery, the Artisans Shop, John Leidys gifts, all in Ann Arbor, plus the Detroit Artists Market. Beginning in the 1960s however, we were able to sell work in our own twice-a-year large Guild sales, plus the Street Art Fair that we helped create. Between these sales and local galleries, more demand for pottery has been created than we can fill.

It is not surprising therefore, that a major emphasis at the Guild in the last 30 years has been on selling our work. This means largely giving up the labored-over, unique one-piece-at-a-time method of working. Finally coming to understand and adopt the faster, high skills in throwing and construction, and repeating of good forms, all in the oriental tradition. And so we find ourselves brought back again to Leach, this time for skill level and working methods.

ODE TO THE GUILD
from a Kiln Chair upon retiring

When you come into the Guild
Take a good look around;
Do the natives seem restless?
There's work to be found!

Don't wait to be asked,
Do a little each day;
Points are not the issue
If the Guild's here to stay.

Unbricking, unstacking,
Constant grunt work in the making;
Volunteers are so welcome
To keep backs from breaking.

Are the carts bristling with greenware?
It multiplies by the day;
Time out for consolidating
Will keep tempers unfrayed.

Bricking's a chore that comes
After hours of stacking;
You'll find if you do it,
Friends will never be lacking!

And if you do help to brick,
Please don't wait too long;
Or your friendly kiln chairman
Will be lighting warmups at dawn.

And then there is stacking,
Tests brain power and backs;
We can lead you to the kiln room,
But we can't make you stack.

But if you should decide
That this challenge is for you,
We'll teach you and coach you
'til you're one of our crew.

This group is a co-op,
It depends on all working,
Long after points are earned,
The tasks are still lurking.

After throwing and hand-building,
Glazing and tooling,
Long after new pots have stopped
Pinging and cooling.

The shared work and joint effort,
Conversations and laughter;
These are the memories
You'll have ever after.

The Guild is your family,
Demanding unselfishness and heart;
For the whole is much greater
Than the sum of its parts.

Gail Dapogny

Mary (Kring) Risley checking the kiln in the 1950s

Kiln room in the mid-60s. (L) Liz Davis. (R) Pauline Elliott.

Inge Merlin stacking the bisque kiln, 2000

The Raku area

The Heart of the Studio - the Kilns

The Potters Guild is fortunate to have seven kilns, custom-built or acquired over the years. Doors to the gas kilns are built up and taken down for each firing with soft insulating bricks.

Kilns	Usage
1. Indoor 54 cu. ft downdraft gas kiln	Fired weekly as a bisque kiln to cone 06
2. Indoor 94 cu. ft downdraft gas kiln	Fired weekly as a glaze kiln to cone 10. Stacked in 2-hour shifts by 2 people for up to 3 shifts. Fired in 3-hour shifts by 1 person per shift. The kiln is warmed up for 15 hours, fired for 12 hours and cooled for 36 hours. A log is kept of each firing.
3. Outdoor 30 Cu. Ft Downdraft Gas Kiln	Used for Saggar or experimental firings
4. Outdoor 12.5 cu ft raku kiln 5. Portable 4.6 cu.ft. raku kiln	Fired about every two weeks
6. 17.7 cu fit "Evenheat" electric kiln	Monthly firings of terra cotta ware and sometimes bisque
7. 3.3 cu. ft electric kiln	Used for test purposes

GENERAL RULES
POINT SYSTEM, AND MEASUREMENT INFORMATION

Guild fees cover the costs of a specified amount of materials and firing. These rules are necessary to keep the Guild financially stable, and are not intended to penalize anyone. They are subject to revision in the light of experience.

A. **PRE-PAID POTS**: 40,000 cubic inches of glazed pots may be fired per calendar year without additional payment.

B. **OVER-LIMIT POTS**: Pots in excess of above limit may be fired subject to the following rules:

1. A charge of 65 cents per 100 cubic inches and one work point per cubic inch; these work points must have been earned by stacking or firing the kilns, sometime during the calendar year.

2. Whenever the board feels that a member's over-the-limit production is so high as to jeopardize the operation of the Guild or to create an unreasonable inconvenience to other Guild members, the board may direct the member to curtail his or her production.

3. Over-limit pots exceeding 40,000 cubic inches per year must bear a green kiln slip. Those exceeding 90,000 per year must bear an orange slip.

4. Pots bearing a pink kiln slip have priority in stacking and firing over green and orange slips, and green slips have priority over orange whenever kiln space is not adequate for all pots offered to be fired. Student pots have priority over member's pots, except for last kiln before a sale.

5. Work points must be earned before pots can be fired.

6. Members must total points by the 10th of the month.

C. **BISQUE FIRING ONLY**: 1/2 regular points for bisque firing at the Guild when glaze firing is done elsewhere. Greenware follows the same rules. Pots glaze fired at the Guild, with purchased clay bisque fired elsewhere = 1/2 regular points.

D. **RE-FIRING**: 1/2 regular points.

E. **STUDENTS AND TEACHER FIRING:** limited to 13,000 cubic inches per 16-week class sessions.

F. **MEASURING POTS**:
   1. Height X width X length. Smallest measurement is 2" (i.e. plates and tiles). Support rings, saggars, protrusions are all included in measurements.
   2. Any pot measuring 1,200 cu. in., not including side projections will qualify as a "big pot" and measurements over 1,200 will be charged only at one-half points.

MATERIALS TAKEN HOME: Materials taken home for glaze firing outside the Guild (not otherwise coming under the point system) must be entered in points book as follows:

DRY WEIGHTS:	10 lbs Goldart	480 cu. in.
	10 lbs fireclay	510 cu. in.
	10 lbs OM4 ball clay	510 cu. in.
	10 lbs fine grog	1350 cu in.
	10 lbs Custer spar	960 cu. in.
	10 lbs 6-tile, GA Kaolin	1157 cu. in.
	10 lbs EPK (kaolin)	910 cu. in.
	1000 grams glaze recipe	400 cu. in.*
	100 lbs stoneware clay	5640 cu. in.
	100 lbs porcelain clay	8404 cu. in.
	100 lbs white stoneware	8072 cu. in.
WET WEIGHTS	10 lbs wet stoneware clay	480 cu. in.
	10 lbs wet porcelain clay	720 cu. in.
	10 lbs wet white stoneware	690 cu. in.

*Note: glaze ingredients are based on a recipe only. Components of a glaze recipe may only be taken home in amounts appropriate to a recipe of 1000 grams.

POTTERS GUILD
POINTS INFORMATION

JOBS	DESCRIPTION	POINTS /HOUR
Board member:	Work	450
	Meetings	300
	President, Secretary	450
Committees:	CHAIR	450
	Meetings	300
	Work to assist chairperson	300
	Substituting for chair and doing actual work	450
Skilled labor:	Plumbing, electrical work, photography, new design, inventory yard work, food preparation, (non-word processing) computer work	600
Lab hours:	Weekdays 4-10 pm, weekends (days/evenings) (8 hr. max./wk)	300
	Sign up before the first class of the week. Contact substitute if unable to cover. Unscheduled lab hours - may be counted to accommodate a student and may exceed the maximum hours allowed for the week.	
Class Lab Assistant:		500
Filling large glaze cans: (points per lb.)		1
Unloading supply truck: (points per hour)		2,400
Clay mixing:	Pugging	400
	Dry mixing	600
	Cleaning pugger or mixer	1,000
Bat making		500

JOBS	DESCRIPTION	POINTS /HOUR
Travel:	Taking pots to and from shows (minimum of 5 member participants) to be divided trips for PG to Rovin's NOTE: have order shipped if shipping cost is under $10	**1,200** per trip
Other work:	Shopping, word processing, public service	**450**
Yard work:		**600**

Use common sense in doing multiple point earning jobs. Front and back studio work not generally compatible.

KILN RELATED JOBS

JOBS	DESCRIPTION	POINTS /HOUR
Shelf chipping:		**600**
Vacuuming, stacking, door bricking:		**600**
Door unbricking:		**400**
Unstacking:	Including shelf removal	**500**
Lighting warmups:	On site and door to door travel	**600**
Firing:	Glaze or bisque	**600**
Raku firing:	Each person in the group gets **200 points per 1,000 cu. in**. fired of the groups figure. Special trip to supervise firing:	**600**
Electric kiln firing:	Stacking Firing	**600** **400/load**
Kiln training:	Trainee (hands on)	**300**

WEEKEND CLEANING
All jobs should take about 2 hours

JOBS	DESCRIPTION	POINTS /HOUR
Job #1A (front area):	Wet vac around wheels, tables, glazing area (do not vac storage room)	400
Job #1B (back area):	Wet vac main studio aisles, wet room, kiln room (do not vac storage room)	400
Job #2:	Clean bathroom, empty clay trap, empty waste baskets, pick up clutter, tidy bat areas, surface cleaning (counters, tables, wheels and switches, wedging boards), clean spray booth, wash towels (bring back promptly)	400

PRE-SALE WORK

JOBS	DESCRIPTION	POINTS /HOUR
Bi-annual cleaning:		300
Sale work (all jobs):	Painting and construction for Guild Sales or Street Fair, Chair of any sale committee, work parties, setups, heating, lighting, decorations, etc. No points for sale take-down.	300

GLAZE RECIPES FROM OUR TEACHERS
Compiled by Gail Dapogny

The Guild has had a rich assortment of teachers for our students, and, for members, visitors who have conducted workshops. We have all benefited enormously from this range of expertise through the years. One special byproduct of many of our teachers is the range of their glaze experiences and, with that, the glaze recipes which they have left for us to try. Since many potters are somewhat territorial about their pet glazes, this is indeed a treat. Some of the glazes bequeathed to us have become Guild favorites. A sampling of our glaze legacy is listed below. The names you see are the Guild's names for these glazes.

STEPHENSON BLUE: from John and Susanne Stephenson, longtime friends and teachers at the Guild, from here in Ann Arbor. A pleasant copper turquoise matte glaze which, unlike many other barium blues, goes to greenish-grey in places due to variations in thickness and in the firing/reduction, cone 8-10.

Nepheline Syenite		45
Whiting		5
Dolomite		8
Kentucky Ball Clay		10
Flint		12
Barium Carbonate		20
	Total	100
Copper Carbonate		2.5 %

ANNETTE'S BLACK: from Annette Siffin, a talented, former member of the Pewabic Pottery staff and frequent, popular teacher at our Guild. A lovely satiny black glaze, very reliable when not used too thin, cone 9-10.

Kona Feldspar		20
Custer Feldspar		20
Dolomite		15
Talc		13
Whiting		2
Kentucky Ball Clay		10
Flint		20
	Total	100
Iron Oxide		3 %
Cobalt Oxide		2 %
Manganese Dioxide		1 %
Chromium Oxide		3 %

LOREE C10: from John Loree, retired ceramics Professor at EMU and Guild friend. A semi-matte glaze, very reliable, that takes oxides extremely well.

EPK		25
Zinc Oxide		8
Gerstley Borate		3
Whiting		31
Cornwall Stone		23
Nepheline Syenite		3
Potash Feldspar		7
	Total	100
cobalt oxide		.5 %
copper carbonate		2 %

K9: from David Parsons, one of our most popular teachers, a recent member who served as our president, and has since migrated to California where he is now working mainly in wood. A shiny glaze which varies according to thickness from yellow-gold to blue tints, cone 9-10.

Custer Feldspar		61.9
EPK		5.4
Dolomite		9.7
Kentucky Ball Clay		9
Barium Carbonate		5.4
Whiting		4.3
Flint		4.3
	Total	100
Rutile		4.34 %
Iron Oxide		2.06 %

CROWELL CLEAR: from Susan Crowell, Professor at the Univesity of Michigan Residential College; former member and Guild friend. A soft shiny white (over porcelain). cone 9-10.

Kona Feldspar		40
Whiting		14
Zinc Oxide		4.8
Wollastonite		.5
Talc		4
EPK		7.7
Flint		28
Tin Oxide		1
	Total	100

WEISER GREEN: from Kurt Weiser, a teacher in the 70s who went on to become the director of the famed Archie Bray Foundation and is now at the Arizona State University at Tempe. A satiny solid medium green, extremely reliable, cone 9-10.

Custer Feldspar		63
Dolomite		24
Flint		4
Kentucky Ball Clay		9
	Total	100
cobalt carbonate		.5 %
chromium oxide		1.5 %

WEISER RED ASH: another glaze from Kurt Weiser (see above). Shiny glaze, can have dramatic effects ranging from cream to rust, cone 9.

Potash Feldspar		44
Talc		3
EPK		21
Bone Ash		3
Whiting		18
Wood Ash		11
	Total	100
Iron Oxide		5 %
Ochre		12 %

WOO CELADON: from Marie Woo, well known ceramic artist and friend of the Guild who, fortunately for us, lives in the Detroit area. A lovely celadon which tends toward blue tones, cone 9-10.

Potash Feldspar		28
Flint		34
EPK		3
Whiting		17
Talc		3
Barium Carbonate		13
Dolomite		2
	Total	100
Iron Oxide		1-2 %

Potters Guild 1949-2000

Golden Anniversary Celebration 1999-2000

Working Studio Open House and Silent Auction	September 25, 1999
Non-profit booth at the Sculpture, Objects and Functional Art Show (SOFA), Chicago, IL	Nov. 4-8, 1999
National Council on Education for the Ceramic Arts "Connections," Denver, CO	March 23, 2000
Preview Reception for "Firing Cycle" Slusser Gallery at the University of Michigan School of Art	Nov. 10, 2000
"Firing Cycle: 50 years of Clay at the Potters Guild"	Nov. 11-Dec. 15, 2000
Gallery Talk with John Stephenson	Nov. 12, 2000
3 Short Talks (by former teachers) in the Alumni Room at the McKenny Union Eastern Michigan University	Nov. 15, 2000
Handbuilding Functional Pots: A one day demo with Gail Kendall	Nov. 18, 2000

Founding Members of the Potters Guild - 1949

Hilda Burr	William Lewis	Carlos Palmer
Wilma Donahue	Harvey Littleton	Giulia Sunblad
Eleanor LaPorte	Ruth Lobdell	Harriet Waite

Members of the Potters Guild: 1949-Present

This is not a definitive list, but a work in progress. If you know someone who has been omitted, please contact:

Historian, Potters Guild, 201 Hill St., Ann Arbor, MI 48014, 734-663-4970.

JT Abernathy	Jim Clark	Irene Fast
Beverly Allport	Debby Cocoros	Sid and Lois Feller
Donna Baker	Madeline Conboy	Viola Fisher
Penelope Barlow	Jane Connin	Charlene Fisher-
Adele M. Barres	Mary Coulam	Birenbaum
Mary Blanton	Larry Cronk	Ryan Forrey
Ann Borkin	Susan Crowell	Joyce Friedrich
Sally Breckenridge	Gail Dapogny	Sally Goldberg
Luba Burton	Francois Dancereau	Charlotte Greenman
Cindy Wolf Campbell	Gail Davidson	Emerson Greenman
Signe Carpenter	Jim Davies	Dina Greenway
Jo Carter	Liz Davis	Nancy Grob
Maria Carter	Royce Disbrow	Gerry Grygotis
Sue Chase	Michael Dolan	Harriet Hamme Shaw
Marjorie Chavarelle	Vee Ling Edwards	Jean Hazen
Mignonette Cheng	Pauline Elliott	Linda Heckencamp
Vivien Chow	Millie Empedocles	Barbara Heers
Mary Chuang	Mary Farkas	James Heinonen

Bruce Henry
Eleanor Heth
Gary Hoffman
Gerhard Hoffman
Lillian Hoffman
Lily Hoffman
Jeri Hollister
Ann Hopkins Borkin
Freda Hulse
Francie Jacobson
Roberta Jacoby
Evelyn Jaffe
Loretta Jenkins
Gail Jones
Shirley Knudsvig
Jane Korten
Eppie Kudrna Potts
Jo Langton
Harriet Larkin
Tad Lawrence
Will Laycock
Gloria Lazar
Dorothy Levin
Isabella Liddell
Richard Lincoln
Ed Lindberg
Ulla Lindholm
Rebecca Liu
Inegard Loehr
Penny Lofaro
Janet Longobucco
Rhoda Lopez
Barbara Mansfield
Duncan McCarthy
Janka McClatchey
Judith McFarland
Betty McHargue

Ruth McKevitt
Susan McKinney
Larry McMahon
Inge Merlin
Charles Meyer
Marilyn Mihal
Richard Mitchell
William Morgan
Ikoko Morino
Alice Mulchahey
Marguerite Mundas
Norma Neilson
Roann Ogawa
Carol Orwant
Joan Otis
David Parsons
Marian Peep
Tricia Perenchio
Louise Piranian
Nancy Plum
Jeanette Powell
Jan Powers
Carol Pytko
Winnie Ramfjord
Donna Rea
Maxwell Reade
Alice Reischer
I.B. Remsen
Judith Reynolds
Daniela Richter
Ann Ripperger
Helen Ritt
Lisa Rosman
Maggie Rotman
Cher Rusling
Penny Sahara
Susan Salmeron

Deb Saravolatz
Ena Schlorff
Helga Schmerl Haller
Curt Schneider
Monnie Schraeder
Ellie Shappirio
Kate Slighton
Anna Smith
Brian Smith
Denise Smith
Charlott Spaulding
Jim Spevak
Nesta Spink
Steve Stefanac
Bobbi Stevens
Kris Stewart
Sue Stoll
Sarah Taggart
Carrie Taylor
Marilyn Thayer
Debbie Thompson
Terry Titus
Larry Vanderberg
Laura Vaughn
Eva Vichules
Gordon Ward
Louise Weatherford
Shirley White-Black
Friedelle Winans
Elaine Wolf
Jim Wolfe
JinYoung Yeum
Donna Zajonc
Chuck Zill